GREAT PETS

Small Birds

Johannah Haney

 **Marshall Cavendish**
Benchmark
New York

Marshall Cavendish Benchmark
99 White Plains Road
Tarrytown, New York 10591
www.marshallcavendish.us

All websites were available and accurate when this book was sent to press.

Library of Congress Cataloging-in-Publication Data

Haney, Johannah.
Small birds / by Johannah Haney.
p. cm. -- (Great pets)
Summary: "Describes the characteristics and behavior of small pet birds, also discussing their physical
appearance and place in history"--Provided by publisher.
Includes bibliographical references and index.
ISBN 978-0-7614-4150-2
1. Cage birds--Juvenile literature. I. Title.
SF461.35.H355 2010
636.6--dc22
2008037258

Front cover: Two lovebirds
Back cover: Two zebra finches
Photo research by Candlepants Incorporated
Front cover credit: Cyril Laubscher / Getty
The photographs in this book are used by permission and through the courtesy of: Getty: Dorling Kindersley, 1, 8, 25;
The Bridgeman Art Library, 4; Cyril Laubscher, 16, 18, 20, 23, 26; Christian Baitg, 22; GK Hart/Vikki Hart, 24; Kathi
Lamm, 30; Frank Greenaway, 32, 39; Reiner Urbaniak, 31; Paul Bricknell, 37. Corbis: Christie's Images, 6; Tom Stewart,
12, Chris Jones, 42. Photo Researchers: William D. Bachman, 7; Carolyn A. McKeone, Exotic Wings Canada, 13; Tracey
Charleson, 33; Carolyn A. McKeone, 34, 38. Peter Arnold: Bringard Denis, 14; H. Reinhard, 27; P. Wegner, 36. Alamy:
www.lifeonwhite.eu, 15; Juniors Bildarchiv, 17, 28, 40; Arco Images GmbH, 21, 35; image 100, 41.

Editor: Karen Ang
Publisher: Michelle Bisson
Art Director: Anahid Hamparian
Series Designer: Elynn Cohen

Printed in Malaysia
6 5 4 3 2 1

Contents

1

Feathered Friends

If you are fascinated by animals that can fly, enchanted by the sound of chirping and sweet singing, and are ready for animal companionship, a small bird might be the perfect choice for you. Birds come in many shapes and sizes, and small birds make excellent pets.

Birds have always been a part of the human story, and are rooted in mythology thousands of years old. One example is the Jewish myth of the bird Ziz, protector of all other birds. It is believed that Ziz is so large he can block out the Sun just by spreading his wings. In cultures in southern Africa, the lightning bird is believed to have supernatural powers. Garudas are mythological birds in both the Hindu and Buddhist religions. The Fenghuang are mythological birds in Chinese mythology that are believed to rule all other birds.

Birds have long captivated humans who enjoyed watching them and keeping them as pets. This Chinese painting of a small bird was made more than two hundreds years ago.

Two gods from the Hindu religion are shown flying on the back of a Garuda.

Certain birds are associated with different feelings and ideas in our modern culture. Doves are believed to symbolize peace and love. Dark ravens make people think of ghost stories and bad signs. The bald eagle is an American symbol, representing pride, strength, courage, and honor. Owls often symbolize wisdom.

It is no surprise that people like to keep these birds' smaller relatives as pets. Certain types of small birds can fill a home with beautiful birdsong. Others can learn to say words. Some birds will even cuddle, resting their little feathered bodies against their human companions.

People of all ages can enjoy having a small bird as a pet.

Pet Birds

People have been keeping birds of all sizes for more than a thousand years. Small singing birds like canaries were kept to entertain people with their sweet songs. Other types of small birds lived in large cages called **aviaries** where their colorful feathers and quick activities delighted many.

Having a pet bird is a big responsibility, but it can be a lot of fun. Once you know what pet birds need and are prepared to meet those needs, a small bird can provide years of companionship.

2

Small Birds as Pets

Keeping a pet bird is a lot of fun, but it is also a big responsibility. Birds—even small ones—require special care every day. Before getting a pet bird, you should be sure that you have the time it takes to care for it. Because a bird requires daily care, if you go on vacation or are away from home for a few days, you must be sure that someone can care for your bird. Some pet stores, bird **breeders**, and **veterinarians** provide bird-sitting services.

A pet bird should have a cage, though many birds spend large amounts of time with their humans outside of the cage. Small birds do

Many bird keepers enjoy raising red-headed Gouldian finches because of their beautiful colors.

not need very large cages, but you should still make sure your home has enough room for a small- or medium-sized bird cage. The bird needs to be kept away from cold drafts, extreme heat, and dangerous situations. Additionally, your home must be bird-proofed to protect your pet in case it escapes from its cage and flies around.

Keeping a pet also costs money. Buying the bird, its cage, food, and other supplies can be expensive. So before bringing home a bird, make sure you can afford to keep it in your home.

BIRDS AND ALLERGIES

When a person has an allergy, it means that his or her body is reacting to something in the environment. The reactions can include itchy or watery eyes, sneezing, coughing, or itchy skin. Serious allergic reactions may cause breathing problems and can send a person to the hospital for treatment.

Some people are allergic to the dust that is produced by bird feathers. If someone in your house is allergic to the dust or fur and skin of certain pets—like cats or dogs—it is possible that feather dust will also produce an allergic reaction. Before bringing a pet bird into your life, you should make sure that no one in your family will be allergic to it. The safest way to find out if you are allergic to birds and feathers is to talk to your family doctor who may perform certain tests.

Where to Buy a Pet Bird

Once you have decided to get a small bird you should start thinking about where to get it. You should never try to catch a small bird from the wild to keep as a pet. These birds are used to living in the wild and do not belong indoors in cages. Also, without knowing exactly what kind of bird you have, you cannot provide it with the right environment, food, or care. The best places to get a pet bird are at a pet store or through a breeder.

Many people usually buy their birds from pet stores, but some people prefer to buy their birds from breeders. Bird breeders often specialize in raising a few specific types of birds. As a result, they are usually more knowledgeable about their birds than the people who work in large pet stores. Breeders can be found through special pet bird magazines, on the Internet, or through local veterinarians.

Rescued Birds

Bird rescue organizations are another good place to find a pet. These organizations find homes for pets that need new homes. Rescued birds usually come from homes that could no longer meet the demands of keeping a pet bird. When adopting a bird from a rescue organization, do not be afraid to ask questions about the bird. These may include questions about why the bird is up for adoption, how long it has been up for adoption, and

Whether you buy or adopt your bird from a breeder, store, or rescue organization, you must make sure that the bird seems healthy and looks like it has been treated well.

if there were any problems with its last home. Rescue organizations are interested in matching their birds with the right homes, so they should be happy to answer your questions.

What to Look for

No matter where you get your bird, there are a few things you must keep in mind. Check out where the birds are kept. Does it seem like there are too

Breeders may have several species of small birds or many of only one species. These three black-masked cobalt lovebirds were raised by a breeder who specializes in lovebirds.

Many small bird breeds are community birds, which means they are happiest living together with one or more birds. It is usually okay for a pet store or a breeder to have more than one bird in a cage, as long as the cage is clean and big enough for all of the birds.

many birds kept together in small cages? Are the cages kept in a safe area of the store away from drafts or other dangers? Do the cages seem clean? A cage that is very dirty or has filthy food and water dishes means that the birds are not well taken care of. You should not buy your bird from that store because it will most likely be unhealthy. You also probably do not want to give your business to people who do not care for their animals.

Peach-faced lovebirds are a very popular type of lovebird and can be found in most pet stores. If you do not see the kind of bird you want or if the birds do not look healthy, do not rush to buy from that store. Take your time to look around at different stores and breeders.

You should spend a lot of time looking at the bird you want so that you can make sure it seems healthy. These two green-winged melba finches are good examples of healthy birds.

The bird you bring home should be healthy. When looking at the birds for sale, check to see if the one you want has clear, alert eyes, and smooth, sleek feathers. It should not have a lot of ragged or missing feathers. Look at the bird's beak and make sure the upper and lower beak meet and are not overgrown or damaged. A damaged beak means that the bird may have trouble eating. The bird's legs and feet should be smooth and straight. The birds nails should not be too long or misshapen. You should also check the other birds to see if they look healthy. Being kept with sick birds can mean that your bird might also be sick—even if it does not look that way.

You should also watch the birds for a while to see how they move around and behave. Is the bird active? Does it move around its cage, eat, drink, or play with its toys? If it is kept with other birds, does it look like it gets along with the others in its cage?

Do not hesitate to ask questions about the bird you want. Responsible pet stores should have workers who know a lot about the animals they are selling. If you feel like the worker does not want to or cannot answer your questions, you should consider going somewhere else. Choosing a healthy bird that is the right match for you is one of the first steps toward a long, happy relationship with your pet.

Healthy birds are usually very active and playful, interacting with each other and with their environment.

3

Choosing Your Small Bird

From the sweet birdsong of canaries to the playful charm of budgerigars, there are many different characteristics you may want to consider when you choose your small bird. There are several **species**, or types, of small birds that make good pets. Some are perfect for those who want to hold and play with their birds, while others are best kept inside the cage with other birds of the same species. Choosing the right kind of bird is a very important decision. You should consider the species' personality, how much space, time, and attention they need, and how that fits into your life.

Zebra Finches

These little birds can live to be about eight to ten years old and enjoy living with other zebra finches. Most zebra finch owners enjoy watching their

You should not choose a bird simply because you like the way it looks. Each species has different traits and behaviors that you should consider.

A male zebra finch (left) is usually more colorful than a female (right).

birds fly around their cage and interact with each other. This type of small bird is usually not kept as pet that you can play with or hold. Finches are perfect for someone who has the time to take care of a bird, but does not necessarily want to spend time handling it.

If you decide to get finches, be sure to buy more than one. Zebra finches are very active and need a lot of space. Make sure you buy a cage that is big enough for the finches to fly around. Because they are so small and fly so quickly, they should not be allowed to fly free. With enough space in their cage and a few **perches** to rest on, your finches will be happy to live with each other.

Zebra finches get their name because the black and white striped coloring at the neck is like a zebra's sripes. However, there are many color possibilities in zebra finches, and some may have splashes of yellow on their cheeks and bright red beaks. Zebra finches are among the most playful small birds, which makes them fun to watch.

Zebra finches are not the only finches that make good pets. These Bengalese finches are also very popular with people who keep small birds.

Canaries

Canaries grow to be about five inches long and can live for up to twelve years. Many people think of all canaries as only being bright yellow, but canaries can come in different colors, from orange-red to blue and white. A canary usually prefers to have the whole cage to itself, so it is best not to keep more than one canary in a cage.

Like finches, canaries are not usually kept as birds that can be held and handled. Most people keep the birds because of their beautiful colors and their ability to sing. Both male and female canaries can sing, but the males are the ones known for their beautiful songs. In fact, some canary owners enter their pets in canary singing competitions!

Canaries—males especially—are known for their sweet singing voices.

Canaries can come in many different colors, like this red canary.

Budgerigars

Budgerigars—also called budgies or parakeets—are actually a small type of parrot. Because of their size, colors, and personalities, they are very popular pets. Budgies can be green, blue, yellor, or white. They grow to be about seven inches in length and live to be around five to eight years old.

Budgies are very social birds, and enjoy the company of other birds of their species, and also humans. One reason budgies are popular pets is because some are able to mimic certain sounds. When gently handled from a young age, many budgies are happy to perch on their owner's hands, arms, or shoulders. Budgies need cages that have enough space to climb along the walls and perches. Most budgies also like to have special bird toys in their cage.

Unlike their larger parrot cousins, budgies are a lot easier to keep as pets.

24

Pet stores and breeders often carry budgies in many different colors.

Lovebirds

These small parrots come in many colors, and grow to be around six inches long. Lovebirds can be very affectionate birds and can usually be handled by their owners. Many experienced bird keepers suggest only getting one young lovebird if you plan on holding it and spending a lot of time with it. If you cannot spend a lot of time playing with it, you should consider getting more than one, so that your bird will not get lonely.

Lovebirds get their name from the fact that they are often seen in affectionate pairs. However, a lovebird can be perfectly happy on its own as long as it gets plenty of attention from its human companions.

Many people like to keep lovebirds because they can be handled and trained. These two peach-faced lovebirds have been trained to sit quietly on a nearby plant when they are outside of their cage.

The lovebird needs a cage big enough to climb around. They like to have bird toys and other things that will keep their curious minds active. Though they do not mimic and sing like other small birds, many people enjoy the chattering noises these birds make.

4

Caring for Your Small Bird

How often should you feed your pet bird? What type of food is best? Does your pet bird have special grooming requirements? Taking good care of your bird is the responsibility you take on when you have a pet. It is important to learn about proper birdcare before you bring home your feathered friend.

Housing

You should purchase and set up your bird's cage before you bring your bird home. Pet stores sell different types of cages that come in many shapes and sizes. Online pet supply stores also have a large selection from which to choose.

All small birds require daily care and attention.

Cages should be large enough to allow your pet plenty of space to fly and climb around. Many types of birds, such as canaries and finches, prefer cages that are longer than they are tall so there is space to fly short distances. Others, such as budgies, prefer cages with tall walls that they can climb. Most cages are made of metal bars that are spaced close enough together so that your bird cannot escape or become stuck.

You want to find the perfect spot in your home for your bird's cage. The kitchen is off-limits because some types of cooking pots and pans

Sometimes cats and dogs get along with pet birds, but this is not always the case. If you have cats and dogs, you must make sure that your bird's cage is located where they cannot knock it over or hurt your bird.

release dangerous fumes into the air when they are used. These fumes are usually harmless to humans, but can be deadly to birds. The kitchen is also a bad place because hot surfaces like the stovetop are very unsafe for birds that escape or are allowed to fly free. The best place for a cage is a quiet corner away from strong sunlight or cold drafts. If you have other pets, make sure they cannot get to the bird.

The ideal bird cage has several perches spaced out around the cage so that the bird has room to move.

Some avian experts believe the flickering lights of televisions are bad for birds, so consider placing your bird's cage in another room or shielding its cage from the TV.

A cage must be secure so a bird cannot escape. Most cages have a latch on the door to prevent escapes, but some birds may be smart enough to unlatch the door. Pet stores have special tools or clips that can be used to prevent your bird from escaping.

Birds need several things inside their cages. All birds need perches—branches or sticks—upon which they can stand and rest. There are several types of perches available to purchase, including plastic perches and ones made from natural materials. Make sure the perches are the right size for your bird's feet. If they are too thin or too thick they will not be able to have a safe and secure grip. Because many trees and plants can be dangerous to birds, it is best not to use branches or sticks from outside. Make sure to position the perches so the bird can reach them easily, but still has enough space to fly around the cage.

SAFETY

If you allow your bird to play outside of its cage, you must make sure all windows and doors are closed so your pet cannot go outside. Beware of other dangers, like running ceiling fans, electrical wiring your bird might try to chew or perch on, and hot surfaces like stoves, heaters, and fireplaces. Mirrors can be confusing to pet birds, so cover mirrors with a cloth if your bird is allowed to fly around in a room. Most importantly, never allow your bird to stay outside of its cage if you cannot be there to watch and protect it.

Toys

Some small birds enjoy playing with toys. Pet stores have toys that are specially designed to be safe and fun for your small bird. Not all small birds enjoy toys, so do your research before placing toys into the cage. Never put human toys or homemade toys into your bird's cage. Different parts may be dangerous for the bird.

Always make sure that toys are clean, dry, and unbroken before allowing your bird to play with them.

You will need to clean your bird's cage every day. Most cages have a sliding tray at the bottom, which you can slide out to clean the food and droppings that land there. Many bird owners line the bottom of this floor with newspaper so it is easier to clean. Letting droppings and old food build up can make both you and your bird very sick, so cleanliness is important. Once a week you should clean the toys and perches inside the cage. Wiping them and rinsing them with hot water should help to clean up the dirt.

Food and Water

Most cages already come with food and water dishes that are anchored to the walls of the cage.

All pet birds need fresh water to drink. Most small bird cages come with small food and water dishes that are just the right size for the birds. The birds' water dish should be cleaned and refilled with fresh water at least once every day.

It is important for your pet bird to get all the nutrients it needs from its food. Many types of birds are given fruits, vegetables, and seeds in order to stay healthy. Most birds do well with vegetables like lettuce, spinach, or carrots. Occasionally, a treat of fresh fruit, like grapes, cherries, or tomatoes, can be given. All fruits and vegetables should be cleaned well and cut before being given to your bird. When you feed your bird fresh vegetables or fruit, remove uneaten food before it begins to spoil. Some fruits and vegetables are poisonous to birds, so check with a breeder, veterinarian, or pet store before feeding it to your pet.

Seed mixes made specifically for your species of bird can be bought at pet stores. Some bird owners like to feed their birds a pellet food designed

This canary enjoys a piece of fruit that has been wedged between the bars of its cage.

Spray millet is a treat that many birds enjoy. You can find this seed treat at most pet stores.

especially for your species of bird. The pellet food, which can be purchased at pet stores, often has the nutrients found in fruits, vegetables, and seeds.

Grooming

Birds do a lot of work to make sure their feathers stay in good shape. This behavior is called **preening.** When a bird preens its feathers, it is trying to distribute oil to the different parts of the feathers. It also makes sure that the different parts of the feathers are pointing in the right directions. Often, two birds will help each other preen the feathers that are hard to reach.

Birds will often help each other preen spots that they cannot reach.

New feathers replace older ones throughout a bird's life in a process called **molting.** When a bird molts, a new feather grows in to take the place of an old feather. A bird will molt a few feathers at a time, so that it always has enough mature feathers to be able to fly. If you see your bird molting, do not pull out the old feathers. The feathers will fall out when they are ready—pulling them too early can hurt your bird.

Small birds do not need a lot of help from their owners when it comes to grooming their feathers. Their preening and the natural process of molting takes care of it for the most part. If your bird likes it, however, you can offer it a simple bath every now and then. Bathing helps to clean the feathers and also keeps feather dust under control. Not all birds like or need baths, however, so check with a veterinarian or breeder before giving your bird a bath.

To give your bird a bath you can simply place a shallow bowl of plain water in the birds' cage. If your bird is interested, it will splash around for a while. When it is done, remove the water. Some bird species prefer to be gently misted with a water bottle. For these species, spray a fine mist several inches above your bird. Always clean and dry off the bottom of the cage after baths. You should also make sure that there are no drafts or cold breezes during and after the bath.

Playtime is a good time to gently check your bird to make sure all of its feathers and skin looks healthy.

Most birds—like this budgie—will shake and preen themselves dry after a bath.

Beaks

Cuttlebone is also a good source of calcium—an important nutrient—for your bird.

Birds' beaks are made of a hard material called **keratin.** Birds use their beaks to help them grasp things when they are moving and to crack seeds and other foods. A bird's beak is always growing, so it needs hard things to "chew" on so that the beak is gradually worn down as it grows. When a bird does not have enough hard material to wear down its beak, the beak will become overgrown and a veterinarian must step in to trim the beak. Picking at **cuttlebone**—a hard substance that many people give to their pet birds—is a great way for your pet to keep its beak in shape. Cuttlebone and the devices that hold them in the cage are sold in most pet stores.

Signs of Illness

Like all pets, birds cans sometimes get sick. Watching your bird and noticing any changes in habits or behaviors can help you identify when it is sick. A sick bird will often sit still with its feathers puffed out. It will not move around much and may lose interest in eating. A change in the color of your bird's droppings might mean it has a digestive problem. If your bird has trouble breathing, or its nostrils are crusty or wetter than usual, there might be a respiratory illness.

If you think your bird might be sick, call a veterinarian right away. Certain vets specialize in treating birds. These are called avian vets. Make sure you consult an avian vet for your pet. To find a good avian vet, ask the place where you bought your bird, get recommendations from other bird owners, or look online.

Avian vets have special training that helps them treat birds. Whenever you have a question about your bird or its care, or when you are worried about its health, you should not hesitate to contact your veterinarian.

With patience and care, you and your feathered friend can spend many happy years together.

Caring for your bird is a big responsibility, but it brings great rewards. As you spend more time watching, playing with, and caring for your bird, you will see that it has its own unique personality. A happy and healthy bird will bring many years of feathered fun for you.

Glossary

aviary—A large enclosure that is usually for several birds. Most aviaries are kept outdoors.

cuttlebone—Used as a treat or a toy for birds to rub their beaks against.

keratin—A hard material that makes up birds' beaks.

molting—The process in which a bird's old feathers are shed and new feathers take their place.

perches—Branches or other similarly shaped items that birds sit on, rest on, or use for climbing.

preening—The action birds perform when cleaning their feathers.

species—A specific type of animal. For example, a zebra finch is a species of bird.

veterinarian—A doctor who treats animals. Avian veterinarians specialize in treating birds.

Find Out More

Books

Algarra, Alejandro and Rosa Marie Curto. *Let's take Care of Our New Budgerigar.* Hauppauge NY: Barron's Educational Series. 2008.

O'Connor, Rebecca K. *Finches.* Neptune, NY: TFH Publications. 2008.

Preszler, June. *Caring for Your Bird.* Mankato, MN: Capstone Press, 2008.

Web Sites

ASPCA: General Bird Care
http://www.aspca.org/site/PageServer?pagename=pets_birdcare
The ASPCA birdcare page gives an excellent overview of the requirements of pet bird ownership, including costs, nutrition tips, and safety guidelines.

Animaland: Bird Care
http://www.aspca.org/site/PageServer?pagename=kids_pc_bird_411
This website gives specific information about different species of pet birds, including canaries, budgies, and zebra finches. It also offers information about feeding, housing, and how to handle birds.

Association of Avian Veterinarians Vet Page
http://www.aav.org/vet-lookup/
On this website you can enter your city and state or ZIP code to locate veterinarians in your area who are specially trained to care for pet birds

About the Author

Johannah Haney is a freelance writer who has written several books for young people, including *Parrots, Turtles, Ferrets,* and *Frogs* in Marshall Cavendish Benchmark's Great Pets series. She lives in Boston, Massachusetts, with her husband and their two pets.

Index

Page numbers for illustrations are in **bold.**